William Tell

Illustrated by
David Wenzel

A long time ago, there lived a man named
William Tell.
William Tell could shoot an arrow better
than anyone.

One day a new sheriff took over.
He wanted to show how important he was.
So he set up a pole and put a hat on top.
He ordered everyone to bow to the hat.

William Tell would not bow.
So the sheriff put William Tell in jail.

"I will set you free," said the sheriff.

"But first you have to shoot this apple from your son's head."

William Tell was afraid.
But he wanted to be free.
He carefully took aim.
It was a perfect shot!
The apple split in two.

William Tell gave his son a hug.
They decided to leave that town forever.